Musings Of A Nobody

Alva Pratt

for everyone I've met who has, consciously or unconsciously, handed me pieces of knowledge

"We waste most of our life
Thinking that we've wasted most of our life."

"If you knew you might not be able to see it again tomorrow,
Everything would suddenly become special and precious,
Wouldn't it?"

"The more I threw away,
The more I found."

"We forfeit three quarters of ourselves,
In order to be like other people."

"I am a year and three months in an open field when I learn:
If there is a shadow of a tree and no trees around,
I am the tree."

"There are three classes of people:
Those who see.
Those who see when they are shown.
Those who do not see."

"If you are given a choice,
You believe you have freedom".

"Between what is said and not meant.
And what it meant and not said.
Most of love is lost."

"You can always count further by adding 1 more.
But no amount of counting will bring you back to 1."

"Love your parents.
We are so busy growing up,
We often forget they are also growing old."

"We need so much less than we think,
And think so much more than we need."

"One day you lose something
And you say: 'Oh my God. I was happy, and I didn't even know it.'"

"Let yourself be open and life will be easier.
A spoon of salt in a glass of water makes the water undrinkable.
A spoon of salt in a lake is almost unnoticed."

"Sometimes,
Carrying on,
Just carrying on,
Is a superhuman achievement."

Musings

One of the stupidest things you can do is have a strong opinion about something you know nothing about. Never tell someone that you understand how they feel if you do not. Think before you open your mouth. You will think that your life is more important than that of others. You will think that your thoughts are more important those of a child. That is fathomless ignorance. Everything is opinion. Do not forget that. Always make a second set of house keys. Give these to your mother. Listen. Listen more than you speak. Speak less than your actions prove. Fill your soul with life. Laugh. Laugh deeply. Give as much as you can. Take nothing back. Appreciate everything. Say what you mean. Do what you say. Speak with integrity. Realise that life is simple. Our expectations and egos make it difficult. Dedicate some of your life to helping others. Everything is impermanent. Do not become supercilious. Be kind. Be kind. Be kind. These are the small things. These are the beautiful things. Everything else is secondary. Everything else is superfluous.

You will spend your life judging others. But feel discriminated against when someone judges you. You are too shallow and ignorant to know just how shallow and ignorant you are. You are too full of self-importance. Observe your actions. Listen to you words. Learn to say sorry. Learn to admit when you are wrong. Learn to say no. Limit the damage you cause to yourself and to others. Tell people you love them. We have the words but lack the courage. You will never be able to tell the difference between a first and a last chance. That is how regrets are made. That is the alchemy behind the ghosts that haunt us in later life. Sometimes you will think that you have hit rock bottom. There is no such thing. Life can always get worse. No matter how happy we become there will always be a feeling of emptiness. Read. Write. Study yourself. Expose yourself to sadness. Expose yourself to art. Learn to be alone with yourself. Many of the most important things in life can only be learned through sadness and creativity. But sadness is not beautiful. Pain is not beautiful.

Education will teach you how to read. Experience will teach you how to understand. Learn a language. It is in doing that we grow. Know the difference between visiting a country and experiencing a culture. Travel. Even if only for a day. Go alone. You will learn humility. You will learn to be thankful. You will see kindness. You will see cruelty. You will learn to be kind. Otherwise you will live your life seeing only as far as you've been told. Question everything. Do not accept vicarious knowledge. There is a lot you're not taught in school. You're not taught that pain is often a soundless process. You're not taught that sadness and drowning feel the same. You're not taught that sometimes people don't want to be saved. You're not taught that words will fail you when you need them most. You're not taught how to fall in love with yourself. You're not taught that you are a work in progress. You're not taught how to be kind. You're not taught how to deal with loss. You're not taught how to be alone. You're not taught the importance of failure. And you're not taught just how much evil there is in the world.

Fall in love as easily and as often as you can. Never compromise yourself. Never dumb yourself down. If it doesn't work. Leave. We are fickle. And we are scared. You will think that you own the person you are in a relationship with. You will make this mistake many times. One day you will learn that people cannot be property. You will think that beauty is a physical manifestation. It will take a long time before you realise this too is incorrect. The simplest people are often the most beautiful. Make mistakes. Learn from them. Do what scares you. Learn from it. That is how we grow. Hearts have to be broken many times in order to be wise. And you will break. You will break down more times than you can count. Understand that everybody is broken. It takes a huge amount of willpower to appear normal. Realise that you are not scared of death. You are scared of what you'll think in those final moments. Scared that you didn't live with enough courage. Scared that you won't be missed. Scared that you squandered a life. Live now. Live fully. Live boundlessly.

Life

To do as you say, is difficult.
To do as you think, is nigh on impossible.

Perhaps the saddest thing on this earth, is the fact that so few people truly appreciate being alive.

So few people are happy to simply be here.

It's a shame we do not realise that life itself is a privilege.

When were you last in love with the bare essence of being alive?

Life, at its most fundamental, is simply a series of sudden and poignant realisations. What we dwell on, do, and share between and after those realisations is what defines the person we become.

We are at our most fragile between these scattered moments of strength.

It will always take much longer to pull ourselves back together after we have been broken, and the parts we damage never fully heal.

Experience life as viscerally as possible.

As long as you do not hurt another person, you are not required to explain yourself.

Do not attempt to use words to describe something you cannot.

Dangerous is the action of attempting to reason your emotions.

We are limited by language.

We are limited by words.

Much of life is ineffable.

Much of the soul loses meaning when conveyed through words.

We can only use words to express feelings that lexicon allows.

Words can only be used to express other words, nothing more, nothing less.

You are allowed to lie to everybody but yourself.

You are allowed to be whoever you want to be.

You are allowed to shed your old self.

You are allowed to start your life at any time.

You are allowed to say as much as you want in as few words as you want.

You are allowed to not give reasons for your actions.

You are allowed to say no.

You are allowed to show pain.

You are allowed to cry.

You are allowed to fail.

You are allowed to have hope.

Both happiness, and sadness, are simply the results of an accumulation of experience, filtered through one's own chemistry and cognitive biases.

The easiest thing to feel, is sadness.

The easiest thing to do, is nothing.

We become what we are repeatedly told.

Often, we are the person saying it to ourselves.

We are our own worst enemies.

We are unaware of our own worth.

All of this is a result of the world we live in.

A result of standardised societal notions of beauty.

A result of insidious institutionalised education.

A result of our own hubris.

And a result of filtered down avarice.

We have to practice how to be kind to ourselves.

We must try to be a little bit more kind each day.

This process can takes decades.

People do not mature chronologically.

They mature laterally, spatially, and anachronically.

We grow unevenly.

Some parts of us remain childish, while other parts become torn up.

Very rarely, people mature near the beginning of their life.

Sometimes, people mature near the end.

Other times, people cannot mature because they do not understand what they've experienced.

It is impossible to come to an understanding of yourself without having gone through tremendous pain.

It is only through pain that we can find meaning.

If no lesson comes of your suffering, then all you've experienced is torture.

Fear causes us to try and stay as safe as possible for as long as possible.

Fear kills dreams.

Fear kills hope.

Fear kills life.

We have been chastised and ridiculed for failing over so many years, that our minds correlate failure with shame.

We will do anything to avoid peering into our soul.

We try to run from our demons.

But we cannot escape ourselves.

We cannot run away from our own mind.

No matter where we attempt to escape to, we bring ourselves with us.

Many of our monsters appear in the shape of our soul.

We will go to any lengths to avoid facing them.

You may think that other people are responsible for your unhappiness.

But you are wrong.

We are capable of justifying anything to ourselves.

Most of us are unhappy because we have chosen to be so.

We are, most of us, too weak to face our own weaknesses.

The more I learn, the less I assume to know.

We lack the self introspection and intelligence needed to be kind.

Simple acts of compassion are never wasted.

We cannot assume our path through life is more correct than the path of another.

There is no objectively correct way to live.

I have come to realise that strong opinions and mental myopia are strongly correlated.

Life is simply an amalgamation of subjective truths.

Many people I thought were smart, now do not seem so knowledgable.

Love.

Love yourself.

Love your flaws.

Love your naked body.

Realise that nudity is not inherently erotic.

Never let anybody dictate what you should, and should not love about yourself.

Self-love has nothing to do with being better than anyone else.

But everything to do with realising that such comparisons are irrelevant.

Loving yourself does not make you arrogant.

Nor does it make you a narcissist.

It makes you untouchable.

It is a strength beyond all measure.

There is no such thing as objective beauty.

There will always be someone more attractive.

Someone smarter.

Someone richer.

This is irrelevant.

Do not compare yourself to others.

The only person you should compare yourself to, is your past self.

We are not our bodies.

The only thing that matters is what is inside of our soul. Everything else is unimportant.

Our time on Earth is temporary.

Foolishly, we work ourselves into discomfort about our external beauty.

When that's not what really matters. It's just a shell.

If you cannot first love yourself, it is impossible to truly love anyone else.

And it will be impossible to truly accept another's love.

Laugh.

Laugh as much as you can.

Loud, heavy, belly aching laughs.

Laugh good and proper.

Never underestimate the strength of laughter.

Keep a sense of humour.

Especially about yourself.

Sometimes people become empty. They try to laugh, but only sadness comes out.

When you can draw no humour from life, then you have given up on living.

Laugh.

Feel.

Feel everything.

Appreciate all of it.

Every sorrow.

Every joy.

Every drop of rain.

Every beam of light.

Every touch.

Every sunset.

Every breath.

Every failure.

Experience the entire spectrum of human emotion.

Be in awe of Earth's beauty.

So that you won't have to do so in retrospect.

Do not live in hindsight.

My mistake was to not feel everything deeply enough.

Among a plethora of regrets; that I did not appreciate everything and everyone is one of the most debilitating.

Retrospective pleasure, I've found, is fathoms less sweet.

There is nothing more beautiful than life.

I was never acutely aware of life's beauty.

People will attempt to sell you things that they promise are more beautiful than life.

But that is a lie.

Nothing is more beautiful than simply being alive.

Understand that when people die, they are gone for good.

Once someone is dead, you will never see them again.

We cannot fully understand this until it happens.

Do not wait for someone to die before you say "I love you."

Death is consuming.

Death is debilitating.

Death is arbitrary.

You cannot understand death, until it climbs into your pores.

Until it wears your skin.

Until it walks beside your thoughts.

Live so fully that death will be afraid to come and collect your soul.

Kindness

I'm only interested in the parts of people that they try to hide.

Everyone is broken.

Everyone.

Anyone who says otherwise, is a liar.

If someone says that they are tired of life, do not laugh.

If someone says that they feel depressed, do not roll your eyes.

If someone says that they feel like killing themselves, do not ignore them.

Do not pass up a chance to extend kindness.

Always be kinder than you feel.

The quietest thing on Earth, is the sound of a person being killed by their sadness.

Life is a collection of crushing ironies.

We must experience loss, to cherish love.

We must fight sadness, to know happiness.

We must starve, to notice abundance.

We must fail, before we can appreciate small victories.

We must see fear, to understand courage.

We must see the dark, to be blinded by light.

We must die a few times, before we can know the value of life.

Don not judge the lives of others by your own petty, limited experience.

Do not become concerned with the apparent injustice and dehumanisation within society, only when it affects you.

You cannot stand for a cause that only affects you, then spend your time judging others.

That is the height of hypocritical idiocy.

You cannot fight for homosexual rights, and be racist

You cannot be a feminist, and be an Islamophobe.

You cannot be plus-sized, and denigrate slim people.

You can't fight for equal rights for your social group, but then turn around and disparage other social groups.

You can't.

Do you not see just how silly that is.

You can't do that.

You can't fight for your rights, but have a complete disregard for other human rights.

Doing so invalidates the causes you are fighting for.

Fix your own silly prejudices before you try and fix the world.

Some of the strongest people, have the most sorrow in their hearts.

Some of the most massive characters, have the deepest scars.

Good or bad, we can learn something about humanity from each person we meet.

Pay attention to what people do, how they speak, and how much light is left in their eyes.

People can be saved with the simplest of words.

For every person, there is a sentence that when uttered, can either save or destroy them.

Many people are not as strong as they may seem.

It's scarily easy for us to forget that everyone else is suffering.

We can never know how much damage a person has taken in the years between their youth, and the person they are now.

We cannot see the inner battles that rage beneath a person's mask of happiness.

Some people wear their mask for so long, they become unable to pull it off.

And as time goes on, the difference between their outside and their inside fissures and chasms.

Perhaps that is what unhappiness is.

When the person on the inside, and the person on the outside, move too far apart.

When the strings that connect our inside self, to our outside self, begin to fray.

Be kind.

Who you are, is the person you've decided to be.

You are only as happy, or as sad, as you tell yourself you are.

Do not let others dictate your happiness.

Only you can do that.

You may think that you can blame others for your pain.

But you can't.

Only you are responsible for how you let people treat you.

Only you are responsible for your own joy.

Only you are responsible for your own courage.

And only you are responsible for your own growth.

Many of the delights, and the sorrows you will ever experience, will come as a result of you having convinced yourself that you are about to face them.

Stop telling yourself that this is the last time.

One day, decide to be happy at the expense of those who are suffocating you.

Regret is the name we give to the ghosts that we create.

Many of our regrets are of our own making.

They are the results of our fears.

They are the results of confusing abuse with love.

They are the results of us not loving ourselves.

They are the results of massive amounts of damage we've caused and left unresolved.

They are the culmination of our lack of internalised faith.

If you spoke to your younger self the way you speak to yourself now, you would feel ashamed.

If you had the opportunity, what would you tell your younger self?

What advice would you impart?

Would you take that advice now?

It is frighteningly easy to think of another person as less than human.

We assume that we are more morally sound than those around us.

We are wrong.

Do not think that because your sins are different to others means you are any better than they are.

Everybody believes that deep down, they are good.

That is highest form of hypocrisy.

Believing that you are a good person is simply egotistic, self-preservation of your hubris.

Never need to see the suffering of others in order for your own pain to be alleviated.

Never have to justify your failure to help another person.

Never use another's weakness for your own gain.

Never underestimate the depths of human cruelty.

Never think that you cannot fall into such depths.

Never forget that you can always do more good.

Be kind.

Be kind.

Be kind.

It's taken me 28 years to learn how to be kind.

Be kind.

Art

Art teaches us that a beautiful thing cannot be perfect.

Art is the act of creation through the bleeding of one's soul.

Art can be the catalyst that tears a mind apart.

Or it can be the glue that holds a broken one together.

It is a doubled-edged sword.

With grief being sharpened on one side.

And redemption honed on the other.

Art is a very sane way of communicating with the heart.

It is one of the few endeavours that has no quantifiable level of skill.

Everything is art.

There is no one art form better than another.

Nobody is more skilled at art than another.

We are not better than our past selves.

Simply different.

Everything is art.

Art isn't simply colours, sounds, and words.

Nature is art.

Appreciation is art.

Kindness is art.

Love is art.

Life is art.

The sound of a violin is no more or less enchanting than the flight of birds.

The multitude of brushstrokes that make up a painting are no more or less important than the collection of mistakes that make a person kind.

Some people live so beautifully, their lives resemble a masterpiece.

Everyone has their own interpretation of what art is.

Do not pretend to try and understand every form of art.

You do not need to be "good" at art.

Anyone can be a good artist.

Anyone can make something pretty.

That is easy.

The ability to manifest one's soul is what is difficult.

Everything is art.

You only need to attempt.

And art you will be.

"Art is to console those who are broken by life."
- Vincent Van Gogh

"Every child is an artist. The problem is how to remain an artist once he grows up."
- Pablo Picasso

"It is a pity that, as one gradually gains experience, one loses one's youth."
- Vincent Van Gogh

"Art is the desire of a man to express himself, to record the reactions of his personality to the world he lives in."
- Amy Lowell

"Art is the most intense mode of individualism that the world has known."
- Oscar Wilde

"Art enables us to find ourselves and lose ourselves at the same time."
- Thomas Merton

"The greater the artist, the greater the doubt. Perfect confidence is granted to the less talented as a consolation prize."
- Robert Hughes

"Everyone discusses my art and pretends to understand, as if it were necessary to understand, when it is simply necessary to love."
- Claude Monet

"Every artist dips his brush in his own soul, and paints his own nature into his pictures."
- Henry Ward Beecher

"The artist who aims at perfection in everything achieves it in nothing."
- Eugene Delacroix

"I put my heart and soul into my work, and I have lost my mind in the process."
- Vincent Van Gogh

"Painting is easy when you don't know how, but very difficult when you do."
- Edgar Degas

"It took me four years to paint like Raphael, but a lifetime to paint like a child."
- Pablo Picasso

"I could paint for a hundred years, a thousand years without stopping and I would still feel as though I knew nothing."
- Paul Cézanne

"Where I create, there I am true."
- Rainer Maria Rilke

"I am still learning."
- Michelangelo

Travelling

When people share their stories.

Stories they've kept in the dark.

Sometimes they'll make you laugh,

Sometimes they break your heart.

At the top of a five-hour high mountain, I sat, tired and alone on a cold wooden bench. Surrounded by weathered stone statues and autumn leaves, I looked out at a sea of clouds as they crawled lethargically through the sky. I sat for hours. At the time, it only felt like minutes. I sat, and I saw, and I breathed.

In a big house in the Japanese countryside, I had lunch with eight old women. We were discussing the roots of happiness. I received the most heartbreakingly humble replies. And realised just how simple life is.

Walking through a large European city, after having lost all my money. I happened to meet another lone traveller. He was French, and having travelled around the world for three years, he was now on his way back home. We spoke for a while. After finding out that I had lost my money. He gave me money. A lot of money. He then bought us a drink, and went on his way. I never saw him again. This was a lesson. Never underestimate the kindness of strangers.

Alone on an overnight coach with little, to no leg room, after having had an argument with a friend whom I loved dearly. I was unable to overcome my hubris and apologise. Unable to mend the rift. I happened to see her again one month later, but was still unable to say sorry. This was a year ago. And now I realise that during the time I'd known her, I had never told her how much I appreciated her friendship. This too was a lesson.

On a continent somewhere on this Earth. I received a message from a person who I had not spoken to for some time, on a different continent. I saw the notification, but didn't read the message because I was out with friends. Later that day I remembered the message. Opened it. In the message, they had written that they were going to kill themselves. By then, they had already taken their own life. It was then, I realised that people die very slowly, very incrementally, and very quietly. Often, they die years before anybody notices. To some, life is a terrible burden.

On a cold evening, in a very, very small restaurant somewhere in Asia. I was having a conversation with an old woman who spoke no English. We were good friends, and she would always stuff me with home cooked food and expensive alcohol when I visited. I'd usually stumble out drunk late at night with a packed lunch she'd have given me for work the following day. One particular night, after many drinks, she began to cry. She told me about things she had seen during the war when she was young. She was releasing pain. I now realise that this a good thing. When we can't release our feelings, our insides begin to rot. She was my good friend. She was my close friend. Just before I left the country, she was admitted to hospital with heart problems. I was unable to say goodbye. A few weeks later I heard that she'd passed away.

In a restaurant in Pudong, two strangers helped me to order food from the menu. I couldn't speak nor read Mandarin, nor could they speak or read English. But still, they sat with me and attempted to have a conversation. After much gesturing and frustration, I realised that although we couldn't communicate verbally, I knew enough of the written language to express myself. We then proceeded to have a full conversation on napkins, writing our sentences down and passing it to one another. I will never forget this.

I believe that travelling, when done properly, will teach you all that you need to know.

It will help you find yourself.

It will answer many important questions.

It will give you experience.

It will broaden your mind.

It will expose the insignificance of your worries.

It will show you what you should hold dear.

It will show you things that will scare you.

It will show you things that will make you appreciate life.

A mind elasticated through travelling can never return to its original dimensions.

Talk to everybody you meet.

Try to learn something from each of them.

You will meet people who treat you like family.

People who you will never forget.

You will also meet people who are bad to the core.

These people too, you will not forget.

Travel far enough, and meet enough people, you will encounter your younger self.

You will see that people are simply amalgamations, variations of others you've met before.

You will see that everything can be replaced.

You will see that you cannot escape yourself.

Learn the language of a country.

You cannot truly interact with people if you cannot talk to them.

You cannot uncover the history if you do not try to understand.

This is the difference between experiencing a culture, and simply visiting a country.

Otherwise your journey will only be superficial.

Otherwise you would have only done it for bragging rights.

To tick another country off your list.

To feed your ego.

Ultimately, the question isn't: "What have you accomplished in life?"

It's: "Are you proud of how you've lived thus far?"

Many of the most important things we will learn, will come from being geographically lost.

Not only is it humbling, but it increases the plasticity of the mind.

So that when you return home, the routine and safety of your life almost feels constricting.

Being geographically lost and being mentally lost are parallels.

Never underestimate the power of mental inertia.

Travel so far that you do not worry about returning,

You cannot begin to find yourself, until you've started to lose your way.

Learning

"Knowledge is knowing that Frankenstein is not the monster.

Wisdom is understanding that Frankenstein is the monster."

Imagine you were taught that the government is there for the people; but really, it was there for corporations.

Imagine you were taught that life is short; but really, it was the longest thing you could experience.

Imagine you were taught that language is what separates us from the savages; but really, language could be mutated to justify the systematic killing of human beings. What if "colonialisation" meant "genocide," "pacification" meant "state-sanctioned murder," and "collateral damage" meant "murdered children."

Imagine you were taught that the only way to be happy is to buy more and more; but really, happiness wasn't an accumulation of possessions, but the desire for less.

Imagine you were taught a standardised notion of beauty; but really, beauty was as arbitrary, subjective, and abstract a concept as could be.

Imagine this world was controlled by propaganda, perpetuated by fear mongering and ran on the exploitation of people's emotional vulnerabilities.

Imagine if all this were true.

Wouldn't that be funny?

Wouldn't that be horrifying?

Intelligence without compassion is psychopathy.

We read books, and we watch movies about other people's pain, and we think that can relate, or that we understand.

Be we can't

And we don't.

Unless you are able to use your own words, drawn from your own experience; you cannot attempt to understand another's pain.

Nothing worth knowing, can be taught.

Everything must be learned in context.

You cannot understand anything if you have not experienced it.

You can never truly know something until you've lived it.

Vicarious living is abhorrent.

We cannot learn without doing.

No matter how much you have read, watched, or heard. You know nothing, until life has shown it to you.

You cannot learn without an abundance of mistakes.

A child does not learn how to walk without falling many times.

A person does not simply pick up a brush and paint a masterpiece.

We do not become successful without having had many setbacks.

Mistakes are wounds to our ego.

But a collection of mistakes, is simply another name for experience.

Never be afraid to fall apart.

A wise person is simply someone who has made an unfathomable amount of mistakes in an attempt to understand.

We are not limited by how much we can learn.

We are limited by how open we are to new experiences.

Learn to ask about what you don't know.

Never worry about looking stupid.

Do not try to cover your lack of knowledge with bombastic language.

Rhetoric and wisdom are not synonymous.

People will see through you.

The less you think you know, the smarter you actually are.

Read.

Read everything.

Read as much as humanly possible.

Read things by:
- Noam Chomsky
- Susan Sontag
- Maya Angelou
- Kurt Vonnegut
- Rumi
- Cheryl Strayed
- Phillip Zimbardo
- Sri Sri Ravi Shankar
- Thích Nhất Hạnh
- Anaïs Nin
- Charles Bukowski
- Shunryu Suzuki
- John Locke
- Sylvia Plath
- Carl Sagan
- Osho

Develop a voracious appetite for knowledge.

Read about war.

Read about science.

Read about politics.

Read about genocides.

Read about history.

Read about socio-economic systems.

Read about human psychology.

Read about loss.

Read about love.

Read things that break your heart.

Read.

Read everything.

Absorb all of it.

Happiness

We tell ourselves these lies,
That kill us so slowly.
We say that we are happy,
We say that we are free.
We say that we are strong,
Then drown ourselves at sea.

A mandala is a large, vividly colourful, spiritually geometric pattern created by Tibetan monks using a combination of many different coloured sand. They slowly, painstakingly, and skilfully create a beautifully designed image over a period of many weeks. And after weeks and weeks of hard work, they simply wipe away the image, sweep up the sand, and throw it into a river.

Everything is impermanent.

Everything is temporary.

Acceptance of the ephemeralness and fragility of life is what cleanses one's soul.

Try as hard as you can.

Give as much of you as possible.

And when it's time to let things go, do so gracefully.

I am only concerned with things that break my heart.

Much of who we are, and what we think, is simply a collection of schemas, biases, and justifications that we have been taught to internalise without question.

When you begin to question why you perceive and understand the world and yourself the way you do; then you will be able to unfetter the chains that bind your happiness.

Be very careful of what you allow into your head.

It takes years to unlearn what you have been taught to think about yourself and the world.

I will not attempt to define happiness.

I cannot.

That is impossible.

There is no recipe for happiness.

There is no blueprint.

No formula.

No shortcut.

No method.

No quick tip.

We have become so accustomed to easy options, that we want to apply them to the most fundamental parts of our humanity.

I do not believe that you can measure happiness.

There is no quantitative measure of happiness in an individual.

There is no scale.

There are no degrees of happiness.

Some cannot be more happy than others.

Happiness cannot be logically explained.

We are either happy.

Or we are not.

We try so hard to hold onto the things we believe will bring us happiness, that we don't see the claws marks our fingers leave.

The more things you own, the emptier your life.

The more you buy, the heavier your heart.

You cannot fill your soul with things.

You cannot fill your soul with people.

There will always be more space left.

More emptiness to fill.

We hoard all these things, thinking that they are happiness manifested.

But you cannot hoard happiness.

Nothing important can be hoarded.

We crave the things that kill us.

They weigh us down.

They callous our hearts.

They smother us with our sadness.

People will try to make you feel like less of a person because you do not look like them, or because you do not have what they do.

You do not have to.

You do not have to be anyone, but yourself.

Learn to ask for help.

Do not romanticise your suffering.

We cover our sadness with flowers and smiles, in hopes that people do not smell the rot.

We are all big at the start.

All of us.

We all have many layers.

But time strips them away.

Fear erodes our strength.

Failure rusts our resolve.

Shame weathers our faith.

We were all big at the start.

But life has made us small.

We shatter like glass, and cut ourselves gathering the pieces.

We are never as happy, as we are sad.

We believe that sadness has no end.

Yet believe that happiness does.

We sit and wait for our happiness to end, but expect our sadness to last forever.

We experience, and remember sorrow more intensely than joy.

This is shockingly illogical.

There are always more positive things in a life.

At any given time, there are thousands of things to be happy for.

But positivity is usually taken for granted.

Expected even.

This is due to the toxicity of our negativity bias.

We expect to wake up in the morning.

We expect to be able to have legs to walk with.

Lungs that breath.

Eyes that see.

And we expect to make it safely through life.

We, almost selfishly, expect good fortune.

Therefore, we only notice the things that bring us pain.

The most important things in life are those that we take for granted.

The smallest things take up the biggest parts of our lives.

Love

The love that you have for yourself, is the same love you will receive from others.

Just as with happiness, there is no recipe for love.

There is no universally agreed definition.

We build our own idea of love through experience.

Through how we've seen others treated.

Through how we've been treated.

And through how we've treated others.

Love is a little like breathing - the more you think about that act, the more difficult it becomes to do.

If you do not love yourself, then you have nothing.

Do not attach yourself to others simply because they show you a little attention.

You cannot substitute attention for the self-love which you lack.

Being alone with your mind is an art

Do not be afraid of being alone.

Only when we learn how to be alone with ourselves, can we be with another person and not need to use them as a means of escape.

Only you can fill your own loneliness.

You must gorge on your loneliness.

You are all you have.

You are the only person that can love you equally at your lowest and at your highest.

I do not believe in romantic love.

I do not believe in such a sensationalised, commercialised, and emotionally draining expression of love through the use of propaganda.

I do not believe in packaged love.

I do not believe in prepackaged schemas of love.

I do not believe in the concept of possessing another person.

To me, that is not love.

Romantic love is an abhorrent corruption, and manipulation of the fragility of the human mind.

Many people can only describe love using expressions and examples they have been taught to use.

I have met disturbingly few individuals who are able to convey their own original understanding of what it means to love, and to be loved by another person.

Love is composed of very small, simple, and fundamental reciprocal virtues.

Many people blame others, because they cannot find love.

When it is they who are preventing themselves from finding someone.

If you have a string of bad relationships, perhaps it's not your partners who are to blame.

Perhaps it's you.

After all, you are the common denominator.

There is poison inside each of us.

We spend out entire lives looking for love in everyone but ourselves.

When we don't love ourselves, we try to find it in others.

Do not try to love those who do not love you.

Do not think that if you simply love someone hard enough, they will love you back.

That is wrong.

That is masochistic.

Sometimes, mistakenly, we see love in obsession, in attachment, in jealousy, and in hatred.

We are, most of us, very damaged.

And damaged people can only attract other damaged people.

Fall in love as easily, and as often as you can.

If you love someone, tell them.

Tell them often.

Make sure you do this, because regret is many times stronger than gratitude.

Much of life is temporary.

Much of love is temporary.

Many of the people we meet, are temporary people.

I do not believe that love is rare.

Nor do I believe that to love often, means to love shallow.

We cannot learn how to love deeply, by loving rarely.

No matter how many times your heart has been broken, you can still love.

We can only discover our own concept of love through our mistakes.

We can love an infinite amount of times.

We can love an infinite amount of people.

We can leave a love at any time.

We choose not to, because of fear.

Fear of not having someone to depend on.

Fear of not having someone depend on us.

Fear of being alone.

Fear of a wounded ego.

And fear of losing our false sense of security.

We cannot run out of love.

Make your mistakes.

Learn from them.

Love can only damage us if we stay when it's unrequited.

Sometimes, inside a relationship, we can become so damaged that we are rendered unable to create our own concept of love.

We adopt the abuser's idea of love as our own.

Giving people a whole host of chances does not make them treat you any better.

People do not change so easily.

You let people love you, or abuse you, through what you allow, and what you deny them.

Don't buy into someone else's love.

Learn to spot a toxic human before they damage you.

Many people are toxic.

They take pieces of other's freedom.

They steal the light from their eyes.

You could be one of those toxic individuals.

Quite often, we simply fall in love with the idea of love, not the person.

A lot of the time, people in a relationship do things that look a lot like love, and sound a lot like love.

But it's simply two people who are doing and saying what they think the other wants.

They are only playing at love.

Pretending to care.

Very few people are unashamedly themselves.

If you feel exhausted in a relationship, it may be because you are giving all of yourself and receiving nothing in return.

We squander our love on those who are apathetic towards us.

And keep our love from those who genuinely care.

The fact that we chase those who make us feel less than human, says more about us than it does about them.

Do not wait until it's too late, to appreciate those who love you.

Be very careful with what you use to build your love.

Respect and kindness begets respectful and kind love.

Capricious and egotistic ideals begets capricious and egotistic love.

Some loves are built from sapphire.

Others, from chalk.

Fickle ideals do not last very long.

When the ideals that your love is founded on begin to crumble.

So too will your love.

If you love someone.

Tell them.

Tell them often.

Tell them boldly.

People rarely feel loved.

People need to be believed in.

People need to be told that they are loved.

People need to be loved so freely that they are able to find love in themselves.

I truly do not believe that any of us wants to live, as badly as we want to be loved.

"For what it's worth:
It's never too late to be whoever you want to be.
I hope you live a life you're proud of,
And if you find you're not,
I hope you have the strength to start over."

6046344R00058

Printed in Germany
by Amazon Distribution
GmbH, Leipzig